From Welfare to Queen

Get off the System & Gain Your Independence

Author: Toshar Bryant

Table of Contents

Having Your Own – A Cold and Dark Christmas..............1

The System/Opportunity Meets Preparation.................2

Building Character through Determination....................3

Networking: Build Your Team from the Ground Up.......4

Facing Your Fears: Unfinished Business.........................5

Staying Laser Focused through Adversity......................6

Live..7

Foreword

Toshar Bryant is a light that shines in the dark place. Even when it seemed as though many trials and tribulations encamped around her, she still moved with style, grace and determination.

A single mother of six raising her children in Harlem, Toshar enrolled them in great schools and wonderful programs as she attended school to educate herself and obtain her Bachelor's degree. She was such a great inspiration to me, as I had found myself on a similar journey many years later. Having her children like stair-steps one after the other, during my own times of trouble, I reminded myself that Toshar raised her children firmly, but gracefully. I thought of her so many times when I wanted to give up and thought there's no way that I can do this. Her children were always well-dressed, well-mannered, and always seemed to have all of the things they needed to make it in this world. According to the children as they became adults themselves, their mom "made it look so easy." The lesson she gave me in that instance was to share what you're going through with your children; don't try to hide things in order to make them appear easier than it actually is. Toshar encouraged me to communicate openly and freely with my children. She encouraged me to create and maintain a space for them to grow. I considered this wise advice. As she once shared with me, while our children come through us and we have authority over their lives, they are their own divine beings.

In that reality, we have to learn how to balance power and control over allowing children the freedom to find themselves, and to assist and facilitate as they start the path of their individual journey. I often wondered how in the world Toshar did it. I reached out to her frequently, and there were so many times that she would give me such sound advice concerning her experiences with her children, noting what she could have done differently had she known then what she knows now. I appreciate Toshar a great deal for being transparent and honest about the other side of what we really couldn't see.

It is my belief that Toshar Bryant has mastered how to move as a divine being on the earth, serving as a host that God can use. She is allowing herself to be used by the Most High as a testimony to what He can do for you when you trust, have faith, and do the work. Toshar has done her work and continues to do so with greater clarity, confidence, and faith in herself and God. Amen.

Toshar has passed her test which allows her to reflect and share her testimony, and for that, we are grateful. Thank you for your courage, your perseverance, your strength, your wisdom, your commitment, and your deep well of love. May the wells of the universe overflow and keep your cup flowing always.

For those who thirst for answers to lessons God has blessed you to learn, may your experiences in life and the words in this book quench your thirst. May those who are searching for change from a bitter path, seeking a better way, find answers within the pages of this book. It is a pathway to a hopeful future and brighter days lie ahead. It is my hope that this book be a source of strength and a point of reference for all who come in contact with it. May this book elevate our knowledge, wisdom, and understanding of why we must go on our journey to get the lessons we need to learn, and to get the blessings God has in store for each of us. All praise, honor, and glory to the Most High God, and the Christ in you.

In Jesus' mighty name, Ase & Amen,

Kim Wade-Ault

INTRODUCTION

Dear Reader –

It is my hope that as you read through each chapter of this book, you will become inspired and empowered to forge ahead in your own journey. My experiences through "The System" may be similar to yours, or they may be completely foreign. No matter the case, I have included a *Journaling Your Experience* page at the end of each chapter so that you may reflect on what you have just read. My decision to name Faith, the baby that I was pregnant with, was inspired by the strength I needed during those trying times when I entered the shelter system. As it was then, it is so now. Within each chapter, the section "Let My Faith Guide You" are Faith's experiences within the same "system".

Sometimes, when we endure life's traumatic experiences, we get up, brush ourselves off, and move on. While this may work for some, I was compelled to come back after moving on and share how I conquered my biggest fear of failure. It is my hope that my experiences may guide at least one person going through their life's journey.

I strongly believe that when we write down our goals – and are willing to put forth the effort and commitment required – we can manifest them into existence. Reflection gives us all an opportunity to see how we can create change for the future, while empowering us to make it happen.

With this in mind, we come out of dark situations as beacons of light and hope for others. Your experiences will inspire others to continue to pursue their goals. I want you to know that *whatever your situation is at this very moment, You are NEVER alone.*

May Success and Opportunity Follow YOU wherever you go,

Toshar

Special Thanks

~ *Kolongi Brathwaite*~ Thank You for bringing Life to the book cover. Your Artwork is Legendary. Come back home to Harlem 125th, We Need YOU Back!!!! Thank You for Not letting the "Life Happens" get in the way of this project.

    Peace~One Love, My Brother

~*Jennie, Jenn, Jen, Jennifer Reese*~ My Editor-In-Chief. I know your (I REALLY Mean OUR) mom handed me that 18k check years ago, but her giving me YOU...Well, That's Priceless.

    Thank you for Pushing this book through your Flu season.

~*Ma Ma V. Prospere*~ Thank You for the Blessings & being the Third Eye for this book.

    "We Love You"

~*Kim Wade-Ault*~ Thank You for being the Sister I ALWAYS wanted. You give of yourself endlessly & timelessly.

    The water is Warm, just Dive on in... Love YOU.

~*Yusef Salaam*~ Thank You for being the Ideal Big Brother. Always there when I call, and Most Importantly, The Voice for the People.

    Peace, Love & Continued Blessing to you Fam.

~Tara Noto~ I know running a program is not easy to juggle. Thank you for handling my career growth with care, empathy, and professionalism. All while looking like a Celebrity Boss Lady.

> *I will always carry your knowledge with me and use it to help others during their struggle and growth.*

This Book is Dedicated to the Gems in My Crown

Mommy

Auntie

Cha-Cha

Patricia-Pearl

Aldie

Baby Fayce (Faye-Faye)

Jun-Jun

Lee-Lee

and JB

Acknowledgements

My Twin Flame

His Yin and My Yang

My Bim and His Bam

His Only and My One

---Adam

I Love You More, and More, Each and Every Day.

CHAPTER 1

Having Your Own – A Cold and Dark Christmas

"All I want for Christmas is a pot to piss in and a window to throw it out of." – Toshar Bryant

I can still remember the phone call that I made to my Nanna.

"Hello?" she said. "Toshar, where are you? When are you and the girls getting here? We're all here waiting on you!"

"I'm outside...with the girls."

"Outside where?" she demanded to know.

With a sullen tone, I answered. "I'm not coming over."

"What?" she exclaimed. "Why…. on Christmas?" she asked in a perplexed tone.

"Nanna, you *always* told me, 'God Bless the child that has his own.' So, I decided now is the time."

As an only child and grandchild, I grew up very privileged. I started first grade at St. Catherine of Genoa elementary school and was very independent for my age. I remember telling my mom how I didn't feel the babysitter's home was a safe place for me to stay while she worked two jobs. As a result, I became a five-year-old latchkey kid in Hamilton Heights/Sugar Hill (also coined as "The Wild Wild West"). With my own house key dangling on a chain around my neck, I was entrusted to let myself in and out of our apartment. School (which was just one block away), quick trips to the store, and going to church were among the few reasons for me to be in the streets. There was also a procedure in place during those times when my mom was working. She trained me to call her before I left home and once again when I returned. I was also well trained on how to handle emergencies.

My grandmother lived three blocks away. Mattie Pearl was the matriarch of the family. The respect for her decision-making was a given, and she was never questioned by anyone in the family. Questioning her was considered an insult – and rude. My family was close-knit and consisted of my grandmother, my mom, her sister, my aunt's husband (Uncle Boo-Boo), and me. My grandmother was the first wisest person that I adored. Nanna or Nanny is what she chose for me to call her because she felt the title of "Grandmother" was too old.

My Nanna and I shared a special bond. I believe I was six years old when I asked her if she loved me. Nanna looked at me like I was crazy because she felt I already knew the answer. "Yes. Why?" she asked. I replied, "Because you smoke and drink. I want you to stop. If you love me, you will stop." She looked at me in disbelief and said she would, and she did. Cold turkey! Of course, when I visited her, I looked for all of the signs and kept a close watch to see if she would slip up, but she *NEVER* did. Her clothes smelled different; she began to look different. No ashtrays laying around, no beer bottles in the fridge. Through her efforts, my trust in her became stronger and I felt she loved me more than anything in the world.

At the age of 10, I started singing on the St. Luke's A.M.E Youth Choir. When I told Nanna, she was there every Sunday without fail. From that day forward, I knew what the love of a parent was, and there was nothing better than a Grandmother's love.

There was also nothing like being the only child and being loved amongst my world of doting adults. Everyone in my family worked hard, had good jobs, and made sure I was well cared for. Their sacrifices and hard work put me through private schools from kindergarten through college. I cannot remember a time when I lacked as a child. Don't get me wrong, there were struggles in between, but overall, I had a good life compared to most.

Growing up, I became the typical hormonal teenager. At age 13, I began attending Cathedral High School. Yes, I was still a brat and spoiled, but when it came to the sex department, I was no trouble to my family – there was no need for them to have a care in the world. I was enjoying my independence of being able to take a bus to go outside of my neighborhood, exploring the department stores and their fashion! I even landed my first job at the age of fourteen, working as the Maintenance Secretary for my school which was also located in the same building as the Archdiocese of New York. The position kept me intrigued as it was an awesome and very educational job.

So, you might ask, what in the hell led me to that Christmas conversation with my Nanna years later? I had to grow up. Reality sets in at some point and, for me, this was it. This was my breaking point. I was fed up with being who I was, and letting my family pull the weight was not fair to them. I'm sure if I wanted to, they would have continued supporting me without fail or complaints. All because my "Nanna said so." Don't get me wrong, my mother also doted on me unfailingly, so the guilt of my actions – whether it be from my naïve decisions or simply being spoiled – had finally taken its toll.

One such action prior to the phone call was getting married (or shall I say eloping?) at age 18. I had my first child at 19 years old. By the age of 21, I had three girls and one in the belly. While going through an abusive marriage, my mother was financially supporting me, and this was taking a toll on her. Deep down inside, I knew my marriage had to end so that I could have a beginning.

With a combination of factors, I vividly remember the day my naïve actions began. After high school, I headed off to college at the age of 16. I was the first in my family to go straight to college. Not only was my family so very proud of me, but they also took pride in their hard work which helped to get me into college. Talk about bragging to their coworkers! Yes, every employee who worked with my mom or Nanna at Rockland Psychiatric Center was happy for "Toshar". Why, they were the ones who supported me during my annual World's Finest Chocolate fundraiser sales at school! They made sure I won the top prizes, like my first 10-speed-bike. When everyone (including the patients, who knew me) asked my mom and Nanna, "What is she going to study in college?" they would both reply, "She wants to be an Immunologist." As for my applications to colleges, I applied to and was accepted by Hawaii University, among others, and they all called my mother to persuade her to send me to their school. I wanted to attend Hawaii University because they had a program specifically for the major I wanted. Unfortunately, my Nanna was so worried about my asthmatic condition (which was uncontrollable) that she didn't want me to be that far away without my support team – My Family.

What I found funny were the conversations my mother and aunt had about me getting on birth control before I went off to college. This was foreign to me, especially since I was a virgin and had no intention of giving it up without being married. That sounds good, but looking back, although my mother was insulted, I can understand my aunt's concerns. If I were to describe my aunt, I would say she was the most educated and intelligent woman I knew at that point in my life. She had an elegance and sophistication about her that was unmatched. I later came to realize that, as her only niece, my aunt's concerns regarding me going off to college were due to both my inexperience copulating along with my naivety. My aunt saw me grow up and had a hand in raising me. Her perspective was valid, and she just wanted to ensure that her investment in me yielded the best returns in my own life. However, to make certain that my aunt would be incorrect in her assessment, my mother persuaded me to go to an all-girls college. Brilliant planning on my mother's behalf, but no one could have predicted what was to come.

Living on campus at 16 years old and being away from home was uncharted territory for me. I assumed everyone in my new world was like my family and friends I had left behind. Friends came to visit me on campus and I was able to go home during breaks. So, what could go wrong? The biggest naïve decision EVER!!!!!! Having a "boyfriend." A boyfriend whom I merely considered a newly found friend from the college area.

Up until that point, my experiences with having a boyfriend or two were good ones because they were mostly crushes on people I had grown up with at St. Luke's Church. Attending an all-girls high school and still going straight home because my mother continued to work two jobs limited me from hanging out – or shall I say, I was not permitted to hang out. Also, having a mom who was well-respected, no boy in the neighborhood thought to try anything with me. Being too scared to have sex because my family would "kill me" was a great motivator to keep me focused solely on school. So, like I said...what could go wrong? Well, long story short, I was raped on campus by my so-called boyfriend. That day was the day my life took a wrong turn. The reality of my being naïve had hit home. I felt like I had lost the one thing in the world that I was so proud to still have because most of my friends were sexually active and having babies in elementary school. *Yes, elementary school!*

I confided in my childhood friend, Earl. He had been like a brother to me since our days in elementary school and was also one of my friends who had visited me on campus. Earl was usually such a wise ass, and I had never seen him cry before. But that day, he cried. Ironically, he also called me stupid. As I explained the incident, he understood what I had encountered – while I obviously knew what rape was, I had never heard of the terminology date rape. I blamed myself for getting raped because of the decision I made to have a boyfriend. I also realized the world was not all "sunshine and roses," which is what I had been used to. Needless to say, promiscuity followed and I needed an escape from campus. I was traumatized by a lot of things during that time and felt alone in the world. So alone that I found myself in a very, very dark place. I had to climb out. Being raped is not a good experience; however, being a virgin when date raped...well, that is a double-edged sword.

So, back to one of many other naïve decisions – out of the frying pan and into the fire is where I headed. I started dating a guy named Curtis, whom I had met while I was on a photo shoot with Earl. I was seventeen by now and hanging out more often in order to escape the college campus. It was through Curtis that I met Reg. When I found out that Curtis had a girlfriend who was pregnant, Reg told me he could treat me better and asked me to go out with him. I did, and two weeks later we were married. Yes, you read that correctly. I went out on a date with Reg on New Year's 1988, and on Jan 14th, we eloped. I was 18 years old by then and had my first child at 19. Getting married before having a baby was a value my family had instilled within me, so despite the chaos in my life at that time, I felt I had lucked up. I became pregnant shortly after eloping.

With my life spiraling in a direction towards nowhere, I left college and found myself trapped in an abusive marriage. There were many times that I tried to leave. I would end up back at my mother's apartment, only to return to my husband and have another baby. I thought it would make things better.

I realized that I had made some questionable choices thus far and determined it was time to make a more responsible decision in order to take control of my life. So, at the age of 21 – and pregnant – I decided to give my family a gift that Christmas night. Knowing my family was waiting on the girls and me, I carried all that I could from my husband's house, took a deep breath as I stood at a pay phone booth outside in the cold, and made the call to my Nanna.

"I'm not coming over," I said. "I'm going to a shelter. Merry Christmas! I'll call you later."

Let My Faith Guide You.......

How to Gain Independence
Some Thoughts by Faith

Growing Up

- *Realize you are getting old enough to fend for yourself and work towards self-reliance*
- *Determine what you need in order to survive on your own, i.e. money/employment and housing*

The first time I realized I needed to grow up occurred after being kicked out of my mother's apartment for the second time. I had some of the money that I needed to make ends meet because I already had a job; however, I was living with a family friend in New Jersey. I knew that I needed to be strategic about the moves I made and where I would be headed next. I learned to survive with what I had. It was time to put on my "Big Girl Panties" and let go of mommy's hand.

Responsibility

- *As often as possible, avoid complaining about the setbacks that may occur during your time of growth; get through each event and reap any lessons that may be imparted*
- *Learn to own up to your mistakes*
- *Establish a plan for yourself to start living, not just surviving*
- *Take advice or seek help from others when needed*

My notion of responsibility had come at an early age because I was taught to always be better and do better. I would call my mom here and there, usually when I was down and felt as if I wasn't getting anywhere in life. A part of my mother was always inside of me – we made our mistakes and learned from them. Surviving was my first life lesson. I wanted and needed better for myself and was in fear of living on the streets.

Priorities

- *You may lose friends during your journey to grow up*
- *Ask yourself what's more important: hanging out, smoking, drinking or getting your life in order*
- *Choosing between school and employment*

I took courses in interior design before securing a job. I tried to go to school, but I came to realize I only had the resources that my mother was kind enough to give to me. After those courses ended, I opted to focus on work so that I had my own money for food, clothing, and a place to stay. I never had time to hang out because I wanted more for myself, and, unfortunately, I lost friends once I realized they weren't there when I needed them the most.

Journal Your Experience

Think about your life, your situation, and how you arrived there. Write down the root of the issue. Be honest!

_____

_____

_____

_____

_____

_____

_____

_____

_____

_____

_____

_____

_____

Chapter 2

"The System"/Opportunity Meets Preparation

"In order to see through the forest, you MUST look past the Trees, and NOT be scared of the wolves, bears, nor snares." – Toshar Bryant

For me, entering "The System" as a homeless woman with children was an embarrassing feeling. I knew my family did not work hard and struggle to put me through school, all so I would "get on welfare." It was bad enough that at 21 years old, I already had three girls (ages one, two, and three) and was pregnant for the fourth time. I was looking like a welfare statistic, presenting a misconception about my upbringing and family values. I felt like I was putting my children through experiences that I had *never* been subjected to as a child. Not only was I scared of the unknown but knowing that I had made a conscious decision to dismantle my own family unit (due to domestic violence) – and have my children grow up without their father in the home – was equally unnerving. I knew there was a possibility that my children would face persecution in society (especially for being "stair steps" less than a year apart), perhaps falling victim to my actions in their future. I was also scared of not knowing how in the *HELL* I was going to do this all by myself?

To top this *all* off, the "Princess" I once was, the life I was privileged and accustomed to having, everything shattered through the humiliation I would begin to experience throughout the process of being on "The System." Words cannot describe the mental process of being dehumanized, torn apart, broken to pieces, and consistently reminded of how much of a failure I was. It was a slow and methodical process of normalizing trauma in exchange for help. I quickly learned how to change that mentality and began to create a "bigger picture" for how I viewed my Future Self. This change in thinking forced me to become laser-focused on getting out of the *Hell* I had created for myself. This may sound empowering, but without the tools to get out of that hell hole, it was just motivational thinking.

Empowerment came unexpectedly for me while in the shelter system. I vividly remember times when my children and I were being transferred from shelter to shelter at any given moment. On one particular occasion, I will *never* forget arriving at the shelter so exhausted from the waiting, shuffling, and traveling by public transportation all while struggling with a stroller, the girls, and my belly. To compensate for the long process, I just focused on getting us to the assigned shelter so that I could unwind, wash and feed the girls, and put them to bed. It was late at night, around 10pm, when I checked us all into the assigned hotel. As you can imagine, I eagerly got the keys to the room, unlocked and opened the door, fully prepared to collapse! I knew my vision was not 20/20, so when I saw the floor moving, I merely thought I was tired. I put on my eyeglasses, turned on the light and, of course, the floor was covered with roaches scattering from the light. As tired as my girls and I were, we turned around and went back to the emergency shelter for reassignment. Back to the long process, but I felt it would be worth it.

The reassigned hotel placement was located on Staten Island, a borough I had never been to before. The hotel was decent, but the runaround and dehumanizing treatment I faced the next day during my follow up appointment at the Human Resources Administration (HRA) office was practically unbearable. In fact, one of the workers suggested I file a complaint with the head supervisor. "Finally," I thought, "someone who works for the system is acknowledging and encouraging me to have courage despite being at a low point in my life."

A myriad of thoughts and fears fluttered through my mind as we headed to meet with the supervisor. "Will I be able to explain myself correctly without being further humiliated?" was chief among my concerns. I met with the supervisor who actually listened in order to hear me rather than to prepare a response. As a result, he took me back to the office, addressed the situation professionally, and ordered that I receive the services needed. He encouraged me to follow up with him if there were any further problems.

Through this experience, I realized that the chain of mental programming acquired from being on the system can be broken. My confidence was reestablished, and I was on my way, using the tool I needed to empower myself...**MY VOICE**!!!

The last shelter I was placed into was the American Red Cross Domestic Violence (DV) Shelter for Women. During this time, I utilized the services offered (such as child care vouchers) and placed my girls in the best of care within decent neighborhoods. I occupied their time with activities, including ballet and piano, and developed a routine away from the shelter life. I also made sure I kept myself busy by delving into community grassroots support programs such as Mother's on the Move, applying to colleges, and attending a medical program with the hope of salvaging my education. Through my newly found empowerment, I developed an attitude of not settling for treatment that was substandard. In order to do this, I had to project what I wanted people to see in me, despite what they thought of me or my current situation. For example, while staying at the American Red Cross DV Shelter, I often came home late because of my classes. One of the shelter's policies included the kitchen closing by a certain time each night and thereby restricting residents, including children, from eating, obtaining food, and bringing food into the rooms from the outside. This proved to be an obstacle for me because the kitchen was closed by the time the girls and I came "home". Being committed to taking control over my life and newly found independence, I learned to never present a problem without a solution. As a result, I networked with the staff, voiced my situation, and requested a solution. The administration was empathetic enough to have the kitchen staff leave plates for my babies and me upon return from our long, productive days. I became my own advocate and it yielded the results I needed to see through this forest.

My "voice" was also able to get me an apartment more quickly than the average wait time while being placed into housing (approximately six months as opposed to one year). It was not easy, and I had to adjust my schedule to prioritize my appointments with school, HRA, Housing, and the girls' busy schedule. This rigorous routine forced me to discipline myself and focus on where I wanted to be instead of where I was. I had to create goals (paths to success), so I invested in myself and bought a planner. For me, planners became my outlet which allowed me to get into a healthy habit of recording everything I did. My appointments with HRA and Section 8, the names and telephone numbers of caseworkers and their supervisors, the girls' doctor appointments, their scheduled activities, and my personal to do list, were just some of the many details that I was able to juggle through this organizational tool. Through the maintenance of a planner, I could now see the direction in which my life was going day after day. The progress I began to make towards my goal of getting off the system was recorded week after week and started to become tangible. I could review, revisit, and rewrite a plan of action. If it didn't look right on paper, I could erase, write it over, and come up with a new plan. Having a visual tool complimented my hands-on approach to learning. It also didn't hurt to still have a healthy habit I had learned in school, which was to always carry a pen with me wherever I went. This felt good because it was something positive from my education that I could apply to what I felt was a messed-up situation.

I was regaining my confidence, and I began to see some type of hope in my situation despite the long journey ahead. I began to feel that in order to get the results I wanted, I had to first visualize it happening, and then create the goals to make it happen. Whether they were short-term goals, long-term goals, or even checkpoint goals to get to the shorter-term goals, I committed myself to the process. My passion was that I wanted to be *THE PERSON* I envisioned in the future. I started to view myself beyond my messy situation, creating a visual image of my life and how I wanted my definition of success to unfold. Every day, I made sure that I did something which contributed as an asset towards that future. I pictured my actions as bricks that laid the foundation to my future. I knew there would be obstacles that would try to prevent things from happening. I also expected to be tested by my process to see if I would give up, and if I did, the lesson would be repeated until I passed the test. Every action had to be deliberate and laser-focus was maintained. Don't get me wrong, it was a challenge to get myself up every day (while pregnant), get the girls ready for their day, and to wake up each morning having a purpose as well as a destination.

    Maintaining motivation and momentum when a situation looks bleak is hard to do, especially during those times when you feel like giving up. However, I knew that if I gave up, I was losing a lot of what I had invested in myself each and every day, within my planner. I began to start my days with a self-challenge to be self-disciplined, so that when my feet hit the floor, any negativity would tremble with fear and say, "Damn, she's awake and back at it again!"

Let My Faith Guide You.......

How to Conquer "The Struggle of Limitations" Living in a Shelter

Some Thoughts by Faith

Money

- *The feeling that you have to present an image of looking poor (which is not your actual appearance)*
- *There are limits on how much money you can maintain in your bank account*
- *Drawbacks of saving cash can include being damaged, stolen, or lost*

During an appointment at the HRA office, I was asked if I had a bank account. My caseworker returned and asked if I was sure because she had looked up my social security number and discovered a checking account. She wanted to know the amount of money in the account. I knew then that I should be careful of how much I kept in my account. Having money certainly does not mean that I don't need the assistance offered by the Human Resources Administration. I managed to save a decent amount in the bank so once I get myself together, I can slowly, but surely, stop depending on Public Assistance.

Work

- *You will prolong your time in the shelter system if you are unemployed – you have to work a minimum of 35 hours in order to qualify for vouchers or receive help with apartment searching*
- *Maintaining HRA appointments can interfere with the number of hours you work*
- *Employment is key*

In order to qualify for a Linc 1 apartment voucher, I needed to work at least 35 hours for two to three consecutive months. I initially worked 30 hours each week for one month, but I didn't realize the requirement was 35 hours. I also needed to consider my children's doctors' appointments, so I had to find ways to manage and maximize my time in order to still work the minimum. It was a bit stressful, but I was able to work more hours at my job for an additional two months.

School

- *A full-time job may interfere with your school schedule*
- *Prioritizing school and work? Well, you must still fulfill the requirement or you won't get any housing vouchers*

In addition to keeping busy with employment and appointments, I started the process of going back to school. Unfortunately, I began to procrastinate, postponing the placements tests required to actually enroll in the classes. Being a parent is about balancing work, school, daycare drop offs and pickups, and so on. I couldn't handle residing in the shelter, going to work full-time, and juggling a number of appointments. Getting out of the shelter was my main goal, but it had its' limitations. I decided the best thing I could do for myself was to get situated with my apartment *before* focusing on school. There's nothing wrong with taking on less in order to accomplish more!

Children

- *The environment you are placed in when living in a shelter can have adverse effects on your children*

As we all know, kids love to run around, making messes they don't intend to clean up. Children need space to run around. Even if it's temporary, they need to feel at home and be given a sense of stability. I wanted more for my children and knew the space we stayed in wasn't home; it wasn't childproof nor was it safe enough for my kids and me. The first two days that we slept in a shelter, mice and roaches crawled on us while we slept. The mice chewed and damaged our clothes, and their droppings were everywhere. I felt my children's health was not taken into consideration while living in shelters that had such conditions, and there was no resolution to this ongoing dilemma.

Motivation

- *Don't get comfortable with living rent free*
- *Formulate goals and set a reasonable time frame for achievement*

People may prolong their stay in a shelter because they don't want a Link apartment voucher. Instead, they would rather wait for Section 8 to become available, which has more perks. That can take anywhere between two and five years! After being in the shelter for a certain period of time, I felt I was getting nowhere and began to lose the motivation to move forward. I thought I would never get out of there. Being in a rodent infested place with both of my kids motivated me to do what was necessary to get out – to give my kids the childhood I want them to have. Often times people don't realize how their lack of motivation can affect their children's growth and outlook. Make sure you don't develop the mentality of settling for less and expecting things to be handed to you.

Journal Your Experience

Ask yourself, *Am I Motivated?* What is motivating you now? If you're drawing a blank, write down some thoughts on getting the motivation you need to empower yourself. Don't be afraid to challenge yourself!

_____
_____
_____
_____
_____
_____
_____
_____
_____
_____
_____
_____
_____

Chapter 3

Building Character Through Determination

"A pen cannot write your story without the ink." – Toshar Bryant

Moving into an apartment development specifically intended for people coming out of a shelter is certainly better than living in a shelter. When you have the power to select the apartment or home that you want, in the neighborhood of your choice, well, that's another venture all by itself, and that is what the Section 8 Housing Voucher empowered me to achieve.

While on Section 8, I was enrolled in an educationally accepted program through Public Assistance (the Credentialed Alcoholism and Substance Abuse Counselor Training Program, otherwise known as CASAC). At 23 years old, I was still finding my way through my educational goals – a pursuit that never has any age restrictions! – and I had literally handpicked my second apartment on my own. The empowered individual that I had become was able to secure a place on the waiting list for the infamous Schomburg Plaza on 110th Street and Fifth Avenue. The confidence that I had gained to advocate for myself was all thanks to the shelter system! It was not long before I moved into the apartment in Schomburg Plaza, which offered breathtaking views of Fifth Avenue, Yankee Stadium, Central Park North, and even New Jersey. Yes. I was like "The Jefferson's", living up high in the sky! Shortly after getting settled into our home, I was accepted into Hunter College's undergraduate program in 1994 and I felt my life was finally on track.

It took a while, but I was also finally able to get a divorce. By this time, I was on my own with our fifth child, and I was facing the fact that getting married, while still a teenager, was not the best decision that I had made. It was beginning to hit home. I decided that I needed to get back into who I was before I had gotten married. Finding the root of the problem to me wanting to get married was the key to getting out of being stuck in an unhealthy relationship. So, I embarked upon a new journey because that book in my life was closed and the healing had to begin. I had to learn who I was and build from that. I was determined not to let a systemic situation nor environmental circumstances define my life. I needed to recreate myself so that I could become that future person I envisioned. There was still more of the forest to get through, but the trees didn't appear quite so tall anymore. I learned to embrace the trees. After all, they gave me air – and I could finally breathe!

There was one more person who had a very poignant role in my life during this time, and that was Ant, my childhood friend from church. Ant was one of many friends whom I had sung with on St. Luke's A.M.E Children's Choir, and he was one of my Nanna's favorites. Maybe it was because he asked Nanna about me when I first went off to college and remained a loyal and protective friend thereafter. You know you have a true friend when life's issues don't get in the way of a friendship; when even after years of losing and regaining contact, they are still there for you no matter what. Well, that was Ant, to the letter. He was one of my childhood crushes and a friend who kept his patience with me while I was going through my divorce, never judging me for my naïve actions. Despite them all, Ant stuck with me, as a friend, through thick and thin. So, after my divorce – yup – we became closer. Crossing that line was a risk, but Ant reminded me of how a woman should be treated by a man. He was always there when I needed him and showed me how a man should protect a woman. It was a start to learning what a healthy relationship was built on: friendship and trust.

By now while I was attending Hunter, he was sworn in as a Transit Cop. "A street-smart transit cop," I always joked with him. "Do they know who they gave that gun to?" I had jokes for days. I can remember the time that a mutual friend of ours, who also sang on the choir with us, was killed by her boyfriend because she was pregnant and he didn't want her to keep the baby. During the time of this incident, my ex-husband had been stalking me, using the excuse of seeing our children as a means to be around me. On the night of our friend's funeral, I remember letting my ex know that he couldn't get the children because I was going to a funeral. Divorce notwithstanding, he still tried to use scare tactics with me when he couldn't get his way. I really didn't go out much, so going to the funeral would be bittersweet because, from what Ant had told me, all of the choir members were going to be there and would probably sing a song during the funeral proceedings. It was at this moment that I shared with Ant my reluctance to go out of fear that my ex would show up. Ant was fearless and he convinced me to attend the funeral despite my hesitation and, under the circumstances, I had a great time that night. I saw many of the people from my childhood with whom I had lost contact; those who not only attended St. Luke's church, but from my elementary school as well. Since I was one of the youngest out of the bunch, they were all like older brothers and sisters to me. Growing up in "The Wild Wild West", you just had tough friends, male and female! So, when my big sister, Sheila (who was a straight street, well-respected, around the way girl whose trademark was her deep chocolate skin), came to me in the midst of the funeral, described my ex and said he was sitting in the back row...all of my good feelings were gone. I began to panic! All I know is that Sheila told Ant and he made sure I was safe before they both headed outside of the church – inviting my ex-husband along with them. I watched as Sheila and Ant left the church in stealth mode. They returned without my ex. Whatever words were exchanged that evening, they left a lasting impression on my ex as I *never* had to worry about him trying anything that threatened my personal safety ever again – *ever*.

    With that weight off my shoulders, I was enjoying the fact that my babies were stable now, they liked their new home, and they *loved* Central Park. It was literally their back yard, offering loads of activities, and their imaginations soaked up the environment like a sponge. There was a lot to do in and outside of the community. Whatever my children needed to empower their minds, feed their imaginations, and keep them busy with each of their special talents, it was done. I continued to locate resources, programs, and activities to balance out their experiences.

    Our busy schedule and consistent routine was my priority, and my goal was to be the first example for my children. The importance of education was drilled into them as it was with me when I was an adolescent. So, going back to being the first example for them, I had to ask myself, where was my college degree? This was the one thing I chose to accomplish before I could demand the same from my children. I realized that I had to make a decision, and really fast, because Welfare Reform was the new wave and I was the iron duck. Choices to go to work or enroll into a Welfare-to-Work Program were options, but I was compelled to complete college. I did the math. Through reasonable deduction, I came up with the answer which equated to me having: no skills, no education beyond a high school diploma, and five children. Choosing the Reform Plan option was not enough for me. It was time to create a New Plan – a Unique Plan; an Unconventional plan for its time.

I was so determined to finish school, I did not foresee any problems because failure was not an option for me. What motivated me even more was that college became my outlet and I did not care what people uttered while I was walking down the street with my five babies. I did not care about the way my situation appeared to people. It hurt to hear people yell out, "How are you going to take care of all of them?" when we were all walking down the streets outside of our neighborhood. Or even someone coming up to me assuming that I was a babysitter and asking, "What's the name of this day care?" From the nasty looks of disdain, to the stereotypes of being a single mother on welfare, it all balled down to the image people saw me as: a "Welfare Queen." The hurt I felt was still there because I was being misjudged by people who did not care to know my story, how it all happened. How I lost my way and was in the process of finding it again. I mean, we have all been at a low point in our lives, or did they all forget? Where was the empathy? Like always, a phone call to my Nanna solved that problem! "What?" she asked. "What are those people talking about? Me, your mamma, your auntie, and your Uncle Boo-Boo all work. Our tax dollars are helping you now. Don't listen to what those people are saying about you." Nanna was still proud of me, and I had to seal the deal. There were many nights when I wiped my tears and listened to my Nana Pearl's wisdom.

It was so cool that I could bring my fifth child (who was also my first son) to the campus daycare while I was in college. Their daycare was *the best*, and I was worry free. I was a part of Hunter College's Welfare Rights Initiative, and its Undergraduate Student Government (USG). I remember one day hearing marching and chanting as I came out of class. I felt so good when I saw it was my son prancing with his classmates and teachers shouting, "Fight the War on CUNY!" When political issues arose and stood to jeopardize the college students of CUNY (City University of New York), all levels of power united, even the babies!

While attending Hunter College, I was one of a few students who had five children and was on public assistance (PA) while enrolled in that school. It was a very difficult feat because the Department of Social Services did not approve of it at all. During that time, PA recipients were more or less forced to drop out of college and become employed with Welfare-to-Work jobs, such as cleaning toilets, in order to maintain their PA benefits. If it was not for the support of the college and its staff who politically educated their students, a lot of us would not have been able to function in our studies. Through the struggle, once again, my character was building.

Hunter became my second home. There were instances when I was going through the motions and had my share of the "Life Gets in the Way" moments, but I stuck with it. Truth be told, it was an overwhelming experience. My schedule was crazy! As I became closer to completing my degree, the pressure of the hustle and bustle to stay on PA, dealing with its hoops, loops, and leaps felt like an added burden. My public assistance case could be, at times, closed without rhyme or reason, and just like all recipients, I had to comply with its demands to keep up in order for my family to eat. A closed case meant more appointments (better known as a Fair Hearing) to attend and being humiliated with nasty looks, while suffering through an all-day wait so that you may obtain emergency money to hold you over until your case was reopened. Risk of rent not being paid, being responsible for going to housing court when it occurred, keeping up with public housing appointments, housing inspections, the threat of losing housing if your portion of the rent was not paid, housing recertification – the list of demands were endless. It was like having a full-time job with unpaid overtime! So, it should come as no surprise that I was hesitant when, during one of those housing recertifications, a worker named Ms. B approached me with an offer to sign into a newly-formed program. I was informed that by signing up for New York State's Family Self Sufficiency (FSS) Program, once I gained employment, my contribution towards rent would be subtracted from the total rent and that difference would be placed into an escrow account, which was managed by Section 8. Over a period of five years, I would then receive the saved amount in the form of a lump sum check. I was apprehensive in agreeing to do this as I thought it would mean losing my Section 8 voucher at the end of this process, but I signed up for the program anyway.

Despite all of these ongoing stressors, what could be even more demanding than this? Studying for exams and having ten-page papers due for classes! Also, the research needed behind the assignments. Whew! Not to mention some professors loved to require research in books that could not be found on the internet. That meant you had to reserve the book (because other students needed the same materials) at the college's library.

Times were hard, the stakes were high, but I persevered. To this very day, I can vividly remember one Sunday night when I was washing, blow-drying, and braiding all of the girl's hair – a routine I did every two weeks so they would look well kempt for school. I had a paper due and had not begun to type even one letter. I was so tired and I found myself gazing out of the window. It was a pitch-black night and all that I could see were the city lights and stars. I considered giving up, but within that thought, I had a flash of where my life would be if I did. Well, needless to say, I pulled it together, finished all four heads of hair, and completed my school paper. I'm not saying that my grades were A's nor B's for the most part, but the fact is that I was so determined to finish college and not quit! Many sleepless nights were sacrificed along with Blood, Sweat, and a River of Tears. Character was in the making here, and I was the Gold Star!

Let My Faith Guide You…….

How to Build Your Character

Some Thoughts by Faith

Know Yourself

- Who are you on the inside compared to how people see you on the outside?
- Take time to look back at moments when you felt less than – how can you improve upon who you were?
- What makes you unique?

It took me a while to find who I was. People viewed me as a young child just walking around looking for a handout for myself and my children. I knew I was much more than that. I felt like I wasn't good enough to be an adult, but I soon realized I am a strong young woman and a motivated mother. Refusing to have my children grow up without their own made me who I am.

Know Your Voice

- *If you don't speak, you won't be heard – there is power in your voice*
- *People only hear – it's up to you to make them listen*
- *Speak positively and it will come your way*
- *Don't just talk to talk, have a meaning behind every word you say*
- *Always be the bigger person – aim to keep the respect going*

Being a person who was verbally delayed at a young age, I not only had to learn how to speak for myself, but how to **speak up** for myself. My mother was no longer around to speak for me. During those times when I was told that I'm a kid, I had to defend myself in a respectful manner because I am not a child. While I refuse to allow anyone to speak to me however they want, especially in front of my two young kids, I have learned the tone in which you say things means everything!

Know Your Strength

- *Refuse to be torn away from being the best version of yourself*
- *Avoid negativity - it will rob you of your mental strength*

There was a time when I didn't know that I had it in me to become a stronger individual. Being told by security guards and HRA clerks that I am just another single parent who "isn't going to make it in life" had begun to take its toll. However, it was up to me to keep my positive energy going, believing that I can, in fact, become a better version of myself.

Know Your Weakness

- *Avoid attempts at being someone you are not (It's OK to have a celebrity icon, but they are their own person as well)*
- *Avoid following the crowd (trends and bad influences alike)*

I used to want to be like some of the girls I grew up with, cursing and being rude just so people wouldn't mess with me. Some folks like the feeling of being rude and rebellious – it intimidates and puts fear into others – but it didn't work out for me because that isn't a part of my character. I am such a nice person and behaving otherwise only showed an ugliness that I wasn't comfortable with. I learned that it is alright to simply be myself. When someone disrespects me, I may have the urge to reciprocate in kind, but I know that being respectful doesn't make me weak; it makes me better because I'm not stooping to their level. After all, "when they go low, we go high!"

Journal Your Experience

What are *you* made of? Does your character represent where you want to be in life? If not, what are you going to do about it?

_____
_____
_____
_____
_____
_____
_____
_____
_____
_____
_____
_____
_____
_____

Chapter 4

Networking: Build Your Team from the Ground Up

"You are the CEO of your life. Build your team well." – Toshar Bryant

Returning from a lecture that I had just attended at Hunter, I was on my way to the Undergraduate Student Government (USG) when I ran into a familiar face that I recognized from the neighborhood.

"Hey, don't I know you from Schomburg?"

"Yeah, you look familiar," we said in unison.

"I'm Toshar."

"I'm Yusef."

"Are you new here to the school?" I asked.

"Yes," he replied.

"Well, I'm on my way to the USG. Do you want to come along?"

"If it's okay with you?" he said.

"Sure, was on my way there anyway."

With what seemed to be disbelief, Yusef asked, "You don't know who I am? "while we stood in the hallway. I can still remember him telling me his story. "So, you don't mind being around me?"

Still perplexed, I answered "No?" What this Brother (whose tone was soft spoken and humble) told me about his experience as an adolescent left an indelible mark in my mind. His entire time as a youth was "lost" over something he did not do, and he could *never* get that part of his life back. After listening to him, I felt a commonality between him and me.

Maybe it was because I knew a lot of people who had committed crimes, but hadn't been caught, as well as those who did not commit an alleged crime, yet took a plea deal in order to avoid a harsher prison sentence – simply because they could not afford to hire a private attorney. However, in Yusef's situation, I felt something different. Besides his honest demeanor, I believed that in his situation, the system was like a form of double jeopardy that I could not understand. Yusef losing his youth while in prison and then being released with a lifelong stigma, despite his innocence, was inconceivable to me. How was he going to salvage his situation? Who was going to help him fix this problem of injustice – or did no one care? So, I asked him, "How did you cope knowing you were innocent?"

His response earned my respect. "I used my time wisely and got my G.E.D."

"Okay, so what do you plan to do now?" Was my next question.

"Live," he said softly.

I still had so much to wrap my head around. To be placed back into society, while being stigmatized for a crime he didn't commit? Who could persevere through that? To be ostracized through life because a majority of your "peers" voted against you, only to be released and targeted by an unforgiving and unrelenting society who shamelessly disregard facts? The negativity he would have to continually endure was gut-wrenching. I wasn't too sure if he realized it or not, but in that moment, Yusef inspired me to do better. Sometimes, maybe just sometimes, the majority who rule against you can be wrong! I mean, at least I had the ability to change my situation and society could no longer stigmatize me as a "Welfare Queen" once I was off public assistance. Conversely, I thought Yusef would have to live with that judgment for the rest of his life – despite now being "free."

    Ever feel like time stands still while so much is happening around you? Well, that is what happened to me during our conversation. His determination to press on, despite what people thought about him versus what he knew was the truth deep inside his soul, truly inspired me. If he could make a conscious decision not to play into a systemic issue, then why couldn't I? I had discovered another commonality in my newly found friend. Even with the negative stigma we each encountered on our life's journey, we were focused on not succumbing to it, nor accepting it, nor letting it define us. We were determined to be conquerors of people's misconceptions.

Upon our arrival to the USG, I decided I had to help set things right for Yusef and enhance his experience at Hunter, so I introduced him to Kim. "Kim, meet Yusef Salaam. He's new to the school. Yusef, meet Kim Wade."

Among other USG icons, Kim was someone whom I had become friends with throughout the duration of my attendance at Hunter College. Kim, who was raising her daughter, was a person who uplifted anyone who came into contact with her. She stuck out to me more than any other USG member because she had energy as powerful as the sun's rotation, and her depth of knowledge was more profound than the "Challenger Deep". After a conversation with Kim, no one walked away with less than what they came. Kim didn't spare the babies either! When she spoke to them, you could tell she was speaking life into a future leader. So, it was no surprise that she was part of numerous groups at Hunter College, including the Shield Newspaper, the Black Student Union, and the Caribbean Student Union.

During her college career, her colleagues from these organizations persuaded her to be a representative for the College Association, which decided how all funds would be used for the college. If that wasn't enough, when faced with budget cuts at Hunter, Kim, along with her colleagues, considered having a United Student Government. As a result, they were able to merge and create a resource center that provided regular computer access as well as around the clock access whenever the college's library was closed during midterm and final exams. Thanks to the group's networking, they received overwhelming support from both day and evening students. In the end, Hunter College approved the petition to merge the student governments, thus giving birth to the United Student Government. Student activity fees were increased in order to purchase computers and hire students to create and run the resource center. The college was able to directly see how their activity fees were being used to benefit their students. In addition, Kim and her colleagues were also able to hire tutors to assist students with their class assignments and coursework. This was networking at its finest because everyone was uplifting *everyone*!

For me, Kim and the USG were synonymous with another organization I was fortunate to be a part of during its' early development: The Welfare Rights Initiative (WRI). Just like the USG, WRI had its founders and network at my disposal. Located on the campus of Hunter College, WRI was the grassroots organization within the school which refined student activists and community leadership through their training. Through them, I embraced their non-judgmental support, sharpened my advocacy skills, and learned updated information regarding the system. I had huge goals for myself and they were empowered and nurtured through WRI.

During this time in my life, WRI brought the entirety of my negative experiences in being on public assistance to a screeching halt! WRI gave me the feeling of pulling back that big curtain (public assistance) only to see the wizard (Human Resources Administration) for what it really was – a smoke screen. It was up to me to find the support I needed: a network of individuals who would show me there are people who have a heart; people who could demonstrate how to have courage while fighting to survive; and pioneers who challenged me to acquire knowledge.

Regardless of whom you want to remain in or leave your life, it is said that people come into your life for a reason. During this time in my life, Yusef, Kim, and Ant were amongst the many people who helped me along my path. However, sometimes more often than we would like to accept, some of them have to go back to the source from which they came. In 1994, after coming home late from class at Hunter, I received a call telling me that Ant had been rushed to the hospital. I immediately called his mom who, coincidentally worked at Lincoln Hospital. She confirmed that Ant had been admitted there. My first thought was that he was shot while on duty. I *always* said to him, "I want you to leave the force because you have a higher chance of getting shot." His retort was *always* "I have more chances of getting hit by a car." His words had spoken itself into existence, and I found myself rushing to Lincoln Hospital. I left the kids with my mother and hurried to his side where he lay in a coma. I was devastated and recalled the conversation I had with him the night before. He had told me that he was going across the street to watch a boxing match with his uncle and he would call me when he got back home. I figured it had simply gotten too late and he decided not to bother me since he knew I had classes the next day. But, I also remembered that I could not sleep all night. Unusual things were happening to me and he was heavy on my mind.

Anyway, while Ant was in a coma, more unusual events occurred in the hospital as visitors came around. His IV bag would fall on those visiting him or every time I held his left hand, he would give me a handshake. I learned from the doctors that coma patients can still hear as it's actually the last sense to go. During one of my visits with Ant, I felt a strong urge to find our "sister" Sheila, and this time the handshake was stronger than ever. So, I set off looking for her in Washington Heights, leaving messages for her to call me. After a couple of days, she finally got in touch, and we visited Ant together. I told her about his handshakes, and as soon as she took his side and held his hand, I saw him shake her hand, too. I felt my job was complete and I had been able to grant his unspoken request to see her.

The last unusual thing happened as I sat in class during a lecture. I felt a tap on my right shoulder, but when I turned around, the guy behind me looked at me as if *I* wanted something. I asked if he had tapped me and he replied "No." Class ended shortly after. I followed my usual routine and I went to the hospital to visit Ant (it was coming close to a little over a week by now). The only thing I can tell you is that his body was still warm, but the place where I touched his arm was ice cold. It was a conflict of my comprehension level, and it was easy to believe he was still alive, although I was told he had died shortly before my arrival. Words cannot express my grief. I mean, I had gone to funerals before, but *THIS* one was going to be too much for me to bear. I painstakingly decided not to go to the funeral, but I can still remember Sheila telling me that all she could see on her way to the funeral (held at St. Luke's A.M.E. Church) was a "sea of blue". One thing was certain: Ant touched the lives of many of those he encountered.

After Ant's death, my grades at Hunter suffered greatly. I felt numb – like a zombie – for about two years. It didn't help that Shelia followed Ant while I was still in college. College had prepared me, however, I *NEVER* learned about the grieving process. This was a huge blow for me. So much so, that my mother had become more involved in helping me with the kids so that I could finish college.

Although it was not a fairy tale finish, my preparation through college and the experiences in my personal life transformed me from a person living without a destination into a more conscientious, accountable adult with direction. Now was the time to cross the finish line, and leap into the workforce with my armor of tools: my network, my education, and my voice. I had been taught by the best and the rest was up to me. So, in order to have a smooth transition, I participated in one of many welfare-back-to-work programs called America Works and the only unique quality I can recall about this program was a staff person by the name Mr. Jay.

Let My Faith Guide You.......

How to Build a Team

Some Thoughts by Faith

Family

- Mother and father figures who are in your life, supporting your decisions
- Siblings who are/have been going through the same situation as you
- Aunts and uncles who've seen you grow up and are continuously by your side
- Distant relatives you can reach out to

My mother has always been there for me through my struggles. When I was pregnant, when I had issues with boyfriends, and when I was experiencing problems while residing in the shelter. Prior to going into the shelter, I spent two years living with my sister's in-law and they became my family, supporting me as I was figuring out ways to make a better life for my child and me.

Friends

- *Everyone is not your friend – some friends are only temporary*
- *A good friend will listen to you vent and offer support – even if it isn't what you want to hear*
- *Count on time away from the shelter life, spending a night out to clear your mind – you're allowed to enjoy life*

I never had a lot of friends because I didn't trust everyone; however, I found a friend while residing at a shelter for women and children. Each of us had a son and decided to stick together for support. We had experienced the same problems, we had one another's back, and we didn't feel judged or less than the other. To this day, she is my best friend!

Sources

- *If participating in a program for adults or youth, who are people you trust and look to for help?*

- *Social media (like Facebook) offers blogs for people who have no one to talk to, connecting you with others in similar situations*
- *Newspapers list programs for those on welfare and/or residing in shelters*
- *Advertisements provide numbers to call – people that will personally speak with and guide you from the time you enter the shelter until independence is attained*

I participated in a youth development program before and during my stay at the shelter. My case manager and job developer helped me find employment, budget my income, prepare for school, and continued to support me through regular telephone calls to check up on my children and me. Even though my family never wanted me to enter the shelter life, they were still encouraging and stood by every decision I made. I've come across other, more non-traditional forms of support, such as Facebook pages tailored to single mothers who speak about their problems and what they do to propel themselves forward.

311 Call System

- *Helps you with any problems within any shelter*
- *Call anytime when you have an issue with staff members at the shelter or even the HRA office*
- *File and keep track of complaints you have reported to 311*

At one point, I was apprehensive of the 311-call system. I didn't believe the problems I had with staff members at a shelter would be resolved, however, the 311 representatives heard my side and spoke with the shelter's manager. When I requested a safety transfer due to a staff member physically disciplining my child and speaking to me in a rude manner, they made sure I was transferred. I am happy to be able to say that I wasn't talked down to when dealing with 311 representatives.

Journal Your Experience

Name the people on your team and each purpose they serve for you.

_____
_____
_____
_____
_____
_____
_____
_____
_____
_____
_____
_____
_____
_____
_____
_____

Chapter 5

Facing Your Fears: Unfinished Business

"You are what you defeat!" – Toshar Bryant

The year was 1999, and for the new millennium I learned that when you fight your fears, you become fearless; when you conquer being silenced, you become outspoken; and when you ignore negativity, you will become knowledgeable.

By now, I had a network of friends, my fortitude in life, and my degree. Also, my commitment to journaling in my daily planner was essential now more than ever. I had my support team working with me. With my newly found knowledge and a support team, I now stood as a strong, educated individual – with my babies – ready to enter the workforce. My foundation had been laid for my Future Self. Now I could see my visions more clearly.

A decision had to be made about how to put this degree that I had earned to good use. But how? What employer would hire me, fresh out of college, and provide the benefits I needed in order for my children and myself to successfully get off of public assistance?

A welfare-to-work-program called America Works shed light on that path like the sun's rays peeping between the trees in the forest. I'm not going to lie to you, the initial experience of the program was discouraging, but only because the support that I experienced throughout college was in no way a comparison to the new welfare reform work programs offered during this time. So, I had to shift gears. Yes, America Works offered me the opportunity to sit in on their trainings and work with a potential employer via a trial basis. However, I wanted more! I felt I deserved more! Being an America Works participant meant that an employer was able to obtain my labor and, after four months, decide if they wanted to hire me. In exchange, I was paid at minimum wage, while my PA case remained open. I constantly felt like the odd ball out of the other people in my training groups, and not to mention when working for potential employers – mainly because I had a degree and felt like I was viewed like I had no other skills nor options. I mentioned my concerns to Mr. Jay, the director. Mr. Jay had a demeanor that matched the suits he wore – a professionally distinguished gentleman who took his job seriously and interacted with the participants at America Works like a manager grooming his artist to make it BIG anywhere! I expressed to him that I had a college degree and what I was being offered at the program was not working for me.

It came as no surprise when I received his phone call. "Toshar?" he asked. "You said you have a degree, right?" he eagerly questioned.

"Yes," I said.

"In what?" He sounded like he was closing in on a deal.

"Sociology with psych as a minor," I replied.

"Okay, good. I think I have something for you. Come in to my office to see me. I think I have a real paying job for you!" This was the universe working in my favor. I thought to myself, "All of my preparation was aligned for this moment."

I can't say it was a fear of working because I had started at the age of 14 while in high school. I had to remind myself that my first job was after school as a secretary for the Archdiocese of New York Maintenance Department, so it definitely was **not that kind** of fear. I will admit that I was fearful of failing. Failing at my long-term goals on which I'd worked over six years to build and achieve. Failing my children as a parent by not being able to obtain a job financially secure enough to support *ALL* of their financial demands – especially once they began approaching high school age. Failing to secure a job that was stable and offered good health benefits. Finding such an ideal job with a union would be the utopia for me as I worked towards financial freedom from public assistance. Fearfulness of not being totally financially independent of the system and my family. I wanted to show my family they no longer had to worry about me – financially. They could enjoy their earnings without my needing some of their money. I wanted to be able to experience what it was like to give money to my mother "just because". Or buying my Nanna something using money I had earned. Maybe even surprising Auntie and Uncle Boo-Boo with gifts for those special holidays.

When Mr. Jay met with me and gave me my first "real job" post graduate from Hunter College in 2000, I started working with the Salvation Army as a Congregate Care Worker. This job was a huge responsibility as I was the primary care worker for chemically dependent, hard–to-place adolescents. I was responsible for maintaining concise documentation and reports required for case management. I assisted adolescents with employment, vocational placement, referrals and interviewing techniques. I also supervised child care worker's job performance within a group home setting and their continued interactions with the group home residents. I had to effectively collaborate in support with team members and adolescents towards long-term and short-term goals for group home members. I counseled adolescents on various issues presented within the foster care system. This was a strong start, and I continued to build on what I was bringing to the table. I networked with some great staff there and gained a lot of hands-on experience in case management and counseling skills. This was the real deal, and I learned a lot about establishing boundaries in an office setting, working with colleagues, and office etiquette. My self-realization with this job was that I was a blank slate and needed growth in all the facets of work experience. Learning has always been an enjoyable experience for me which, in turn, helps me retain more information. However, this Salvation Army job challenged me to demand more from myself.

    Play time was over. I knew that divine intervention was involved here because during my brief time with the organization, my co-workers continually asked "How are you being tried through your work experiences here at The Army? By blood or fire?" I asked someone why that question kept being posed to me. They laughed and told me that "Blood and Fire" was the agency's motto. The "blood" represents the blood shed by Jesus on the cross, to save all people. The "fire" represents the Holy Spirit which purifies believers. I thought the motto was an interesting analogy to my growth in the workforce and in my life. When I was asked again about being tried by Blood or Fire, I would answer, "*Both*!" I remained employed with The Salvation Army for a little over a year before moving on to my next employment venture.

Through my work with The Salvation Army, I was able to network with other agencies. I made it my ultimate goal to find value in everything I did so that, hopefully, it could all tie in, complementing one another so when I needed to bring all my experiences together, nothing was wasted; each experience would build on the other. This was applicable in both my personal life and work life. Everything I did had a value, like a handyman's tool. I could store each experience in my "tool box" and use it when needed.

Inching out of this dense forest was how I was starting to see life moving forward. I remembered being taught this concept in high school where one should be a "Renaissance Man"; a person who was well-rounded on a variety of topics, experiences, facts, etc.

With their vast knowledge, a person would continue to build on that and apply that knowledge in life. This is how I decided to approach my working career as well. I was not going to stress about what I wanted to be "when I grew up". I felt that whatever my mission in life, I would accept the challenge and flow where "the universe" lead me. I just had to do my part to listen and look for the signs of opportunity.

Since I had already established myself during my time with The Salvation Army, people were already familiar with me and my work ethics. It wasn't *too* difficult for me to land a job as a foster care worker with New York Foundling Hospital. Once again, I was proud to bring my acquired skills from my previous employer to the forefront with my new employer. I also took pride in trying to learn about some of the history of each agency I worked with. New York Foundling was quite impressive, especially the display of their legacy with pictures lining the walls as you entered their building. What stuck out for me was that in its early years, New York Foundling was a safe haven for babies who were literally left at the

Foundling's entrance by parents who could not take care of them. While employed with them as a foster care worker in 2001, I was told that babies could still be taken there to go through the adoption process. I took pride in working with this agency and was encouraged to build on my experiences.

By now, I had learned quite a few self-inventory employment techniques. For instance, as soon as you are hired for a job, start updating your resume. This is always a good habit to maintain, and I kept a copy on me at all times because you never know who you may meet in passing and where opportunity awaits.

Let My Faith Guide You.......

How to Face Your Fears

Some Thoughts by Faith

Failure

- You live and you learn – don't beat yourself up when you don't succeed the first time
- Take the negative thoughts and make them positive
- You are not the only person in your situation

My biggest fear is failure. When I was forced to learn how to survive, I didn't have one clue as to what I should do and where I should go. After learning I was pregnant for the first time, I didn't know if I was capable of taking care of the baby. I pulled myself together, refusing to fail and let my child down. I didn't want to disappoint my family, being that one child who lives in the street, homeless with a baby. I continuously prayed for better and I surrounded myself with the positive people in my life.

Independence

- *Will you be able to handle the responsibilities coming your way?*
- *Will there be enough money to pay bills and living expenses (rent, food, childcare, etc.)?*
- *Will family continue to help or will they feel you are capable of solely managing your independence?*

Living in the shelter with both of my kids was the second step in becoming independent. I always feared not having enough for my kids – enough money, space, time, and motivation. My family was around, helping occasionally, but I remained at the shelter with my babies. It was my responsibility to take care of my children by maintaining a job, enrolling them in daycare, and working towards a better life.

Moving forward

- *What is your next step once off public assistance?*
- *What can you tackle now that you were previously unable to do while on public assistance?*
- *Freedom from the burden of feeling less than or like a statistic*

I fear that once I am off public assistance, attending school and moving into my own space will be difficult. Although you are entitled to more resources and more help when on public assistance, I feel more sure-footed and confident about being on my own. Once you're no longer dependent on public assistance, you can live freely, spending nights or weeks out with family and friends, traveling and taking vacations. You can go to school! Buy a car! You no longer have to fear being told what you can and cannot do!

Journal Your Experience

What are your fears?

_____

_____

_____

_____

_____

_____

_____

_____

_____

_____

_____

_____

_____

_____

_____

_____

Chapter 6

Staying Laser Focused Through Adversity

"Don't be THAT person without a destination!" – Toshar Bryant

Having all of my successes up to that period, I felt I still had some ways to get to total financial freedom from public assistance. Section 8 was still a form of public assistance, although I was no longer getting food stamps, and now had my own health coverage through my employer. Although I did not have appointments with the Human Resources Administration, I still had Section 8 appointments to maintain while employed. So, off I went to one such appointment before going to work that morning at New York Foundling. It was September 11, 2001, and I had a 9am appointment. I was on the train, looking forward to going to the Borders bookstore located in the World Trade Center. I had developed this habit as a means of rewarding myself after my Section 8 appointments.

This particular morning felt no different. Even after the conductor made an announcement stating the train ahead of us was stuck in the World Trade Center station and everyone had to get off at the Bowling Green station, I was making good time and felt no worries about being late. I exited the Bowling Green station only to see people looking up at one of the "twins" as I called them (because the towers reminded me of the Schomburg Plaza twin buildings where I lived). The streets were filled with people and I asked someone what was going on. I was told that a plane "fell out of the sky." I considered this likely because John F. Kennedy Jr.'s plane had crashed the year before, and another plane had crashed into a New York City building prior to that. I didn't think much of it and continued walking to 25 Beaver Street for my appointment.

I got on the elevator and noticed that anyone who got on or off was calm, as if they were oblivious as to what was happening outside. Then I remembered this was New York and we New Yorkers are not easily shaken. Finally, the elevator doors opened for the Section 8 office. Upon entering the office, everyone had their radio stations tuned to one channel and I could hear the news coming in stereo. The staff was very familiar with me by this time, so I told them what was going on outside, and they described what they saw and felt as the events began to unfold outside. They were aware of my appointment, but I asked for Ms. B so that I could reschedule it. Ms. B looked confused about what was actually happening outside versus what was being depicted on the radio – in fact, everyone in the office knew what was unfolding before them was far direr than the media reports. I rescheduled my appointment as we figured it was the best thing to do in that moment. Ms. B, who I felt was like a second mother to me due to her infinite guidance and the wisdom-imparting sessions during my Section 8 appointments, continued to look bewildered. It was like seeing a parent panic when they are your reference of strength and comfort. Sensing her emotions, I ran out of the office and back toward the elevator banks!

That elevator felt like it was going nowhere and of course it stopped on every other floor only for one person to get in. I remember a man getting in the elevator at one floor and going to the next. When he got in the elevator, I was balled up in a corner screaming, and I'm not too sure if he got off at the next floor because of me or if that was the floor he was going to anyway. The next thing I knew, I heard a loud crash, and the entire building was shaking. When the elevator door finally opened, I ran for my life. The crowd outside was now in utter chaos. People were running in all directions. I didn't know what to do. I tried using my cell phone to call my job and tell them of my dilemma, but it was not working. I tried to call my kids' school and my mother, but my cell phone was still going in and out of signal. I ran to a long line of people waiting for the pay phone. As I looked up at the sky, I could now see smoke coming from both of the "twins". I thought it best to call someone to let them know where I was because the kids were still at school and I needed someone to get them home safely. Now I could feel this was a bigger issue and it didn't involve planes just "falling out of the sky". It felt like hours went by until I was finally able to call my support team (which consisted of my mother and the close friends helping me with the kids). They were worried about me and took on the responsibility of calling my job and getting the kids back home safely. Their tone sounded like it would be the last time they talked to me and I felt the same way, too. My family told me not to worry about the kids and to "just make it home."

Now that my top two priorities were stabilized, it was time to get the hell out of there! With my mind clear from worries about my children and my job, which I still needed, I was able to see the chaos with fresh eyes. I saw different types of people: those who were running from the "twins" and those who appeared to be wandering away from the "twins" covered in dirt, looking disheveled in their business attire. However, what I remember *the most* were the fire trucks heading towards the "twins". The fire trucks and the firemen looked like gallant warriors ready to go into battle. The first truck I saw looked like a ghostly aberration, and I felt as though it was their last time in battle. I said a prayer with hopes that they were safe while performing their duties. I took time to look up again, and I saw charred documents floating down on the crowd and myself. I picked one up, looked at it, and surmised that the person who created it was very intelligent, educated enough to have created the document, and they had a deadline. I respectfully put down the paper because it did not belong to me. I looked up once more, and thought I saw file cabinets falling out of the windows, though it was hard to tell because it was coming from so high up. That, I thought, explains why there were so many papers falling down from the sky. Other people gathered and tried to figure out what was going on as well. We all talked amongst ourselves and I expressed that I thought people were trying to break the windows with the file cabinets in order to get some ventilation from the fire inside the towers. A voice from the crowd gently corrected me and said they had been standing there for some time, and that I wasn't seeing file cabinets – I was seeing people. After hearing that I can only remember screaming, "The people! The people!" I looked up into the sky with a different perspective and was now crying uncontrollably for the people.

I decided to walk away from the scene and get out of the area the best I knew how. But the crowd just took me in different directions. With everything going on, people were running everywhere, and it was hard to tell which way was the safest to go. At this point, I was running and hyperventilating badly. The only thing I could do was hug a light post. I remember thinking I was going to die from an asthma attack. Keeping still was my focus now, but it was not working, and my heart was pounding in my chest. I yelled out loud asking for someone to help me, but all I could see were people running over each other trying to save themselves. One last time I yelled, "Can someone PLEASE HELP ME!!!"

Out of the crowd, came a stranger's voice. "Hey kid...what's the matter?"

"I can't breathe. I am having an asthma attack."

"Okay kid, I'm gonna get you outta here! Let go of that pole and let's go!" Trying to calm me down, he asked "What's your name kid?"

"My name is Toshar," I replied.

"Okay, Toshar. My name is Joey and we're gonna get outta here alive," he assured me with his thick Italian accent.

What came next was life changing. We had reached the end of what felt like the longest city block and we could hear a woman screeching from the top of her lungs. The acoustics within the blocks of that area were like a chamber for music. We started to quickly run down the block because it sounded like she was badly injured. The noise from the crowd around us started to become almost silent because the sound that was emitting out of *her* mouth was so eerie. People began to run to the corner to see what was going on as well. Joey and I finally reached the end of the block and were perfectly aligned with this one particular street looking straight down to the block of "twins". We could now see the woman (who was still screeching). The crowd running towards her looked like a scene from a zombie movie.

What followed would stay with me forever. I heard a sound unlike any other to this very day. The only words befitting to compare this sound to is a cascading waterfall of metal and glass that filled the entire sky. The sky looked like it was raining crystals.

By this time, I was trying to lower my heart rate by walking and taking slow, controlled breaths only to hear Joey say, "Hey kid, we gotta run now!"

"*WHAT!*" I asked incredulously. "To where? The only thing facing in our direction is the Hudson River!" I exclaimed.

"We might have to jump in, kid. Can you swim?"

"I'll try," I said.

Before we made that choice, a ball of beige smoke rolled like a giant tumble weed through the city's blocks, covering us in soot. The noise stopped. More noises came thereafter as the crowd size increased. The military and police were working to help the crowd walk as far away from the area as possible. Joey and I were able to take our time walking around and could hear updates of incidents happening in other states coming from the radios of the military staff.

After some distance, I was able to call home and let everyone know that I was safe. It was good to know that the kids were safe, too. I called my Nanna and she was so excited to hear from me. She had been told where I was and by now heard what was going on via the television. She told me that my Uncle Boo-Boo was scheduled to have a meeting in one of the towers, but he was running late. Very thankful for the many Blessings I had received that day, I introduced Nanna to my newly found friend, Joey, and she thanked him profusely for saving her "only Granddaughter".

Joey and I exchanged numbers and I walked with him to his wife's job. It took me a while to walk home from there, but I was taking my time getting to my destination. During my walk, I had time to think about my life and how far I had come in reaching my long-term goals. If I had died that day, would Nanny be proud of my accomplishments thus far? I felt good about myself and when I finally arrived home, I greeted the kids (who were very happy to see me and had tears in their eyes), thanked my mother for always being there for me, and I created another goal to incorporate in my destination throughout life – I would call Joey every year on 9/11 and thank him for being my "Guardian Angel".

Let My Faith Guide You.......

How to Stay Laser Focused
Some Thoughts by Faith

Strength

- *You have to remain strong to get through any distress, obstacles, or hardships*
- *Keep your head held high no matter what is going on*

As I already mentioned, I didn't think I was strong enough to get through the hardships and downfalls that I was experiencing. I felt alone, depressed, and was ready to give into the distress and sadness. However, I couldn't do that because I have two babies looking up to me. If I couldn't be strong, they would suffer! Living in the shelter and being on welfare seems to make people stuck – perhaps because some of the welfare staff and caseworkers only appear to want to help when, in fact, they are indifferent regarding your success. Aside from myself, no one will truly care about my kids or me, so it is up to me to continue forward to give them the best!

Power

- *We forget that power is a force that we can create*
- *There is a higher power out there whether you believe it or not – trust it, let it guide you through the storms*
- *Prayer goes a long way for those who believe **and** don't believe – pray that you're grateful, given strength, and have the power to move on*

When I told myself "I give up!", I felt a heavy load on my shoulders. When I convinced myself that nothing will ever go right, that's when everything started to go wrong. I had to stop feeding into the negative thoughts. I started thinking positively, outwardly saying "Good will come!", and it did. I prayed every night with both of my kids and asked God to make a way for us, to help me maintain precision-like focus so that I remain on track, and for anything harmful to stay away. Even on nights when I didn't pray, I would say, "The best has yet to come. I have to keep going."

Be Smart

- Don't listen to everything everyone says, especially if they aren't rooting for you
- Learn from what you are going through, so you can prevent it from happening again

I had to be smart about taking advice from people I barely knew – especially if their advice would only be a step down from my progress. Saving money was also imperative because I have children who still need to have a fun childhood (and clothes since mice and roaches had ruined them). I'm not into expensive things and I know how to budget, but at one point I still felt the need to dress decently enough to not be judged. I know this may be a cliché, but you really don't have to be like everyone else. Spending more money in an attempt to fit in may be preventing you from saving sufficiently for the future once you are living on your own.

Life happens, but I refuse to put myself back in the same situation because it only goes to show I am unmotivated, not trying to learn from my past missteps, and I am simply wasting my time.

Journal Your Experience

What is your destination? Why?

_____
_____
_____
_____
_____
_____
_____
_____
_____
_____
_____
_____
_____
_____

CHAPTER 7

Live

"Always stay hungry for opportunity. THIS will align you with seeing it come your way so YOU can LIVE." – Toshar Bryant

The year was 2002, and I was becoming a pro at climbing the employment ladder. Keeping my ear to the ground, along with my arsenal of networks that I had developed over the years, was proving beneficial. I was getting leads for employment opportunities and taking city and state exams for jobs that paid more money and offered greater benefits. It was not long before I was called to work for the Administration for Children's Services (ACS). This was a job with New York City, and it provided all of the perks I was looking for in the utopia of jobs which I had envisioned when becoming totally independent of public assistance. By comparison, I was experienced enough to know that private agencies refined you because you could be fired at any time, without any reason, which forces you to "keep up the good work". City jobs, well, they had a different culture, but I had been well trained through private agencies, so my work ethics and values stayed with me and were not malleable.

Through employment with ACS, I learned a lot about retirement savings in different funds. I enjoyed the challenges ACS had to offer, including learning about the child safety laws in which I was responsible for ensuring. I mean, this job was in a bigger league than the others because I actually had to go through a training academy and pass another test in order to keep the job offer. After passing the academy, I was hired to investigate reports of abuse and neglect, in addition to making immediate responses to assess the safety of children. In some cases, I had to assist families in need through referrals for counseling, drug rehabilitation programs, and other preventive services after an appropriate assessment was made.

As I had learned in the past, every job is unique and sometimes you are faced with ethical decisions which challenge your integrity. In life, we are presented with tests and decisions which will lead us in a direction based on the choices we make –

and it does not discriminate on the basis of whether or not you are employed. This was one time I was faced with such a dilemma. It was as if I was being tested to see what meant more to me, the wealth or the source that blessed me with the wealth. With wealth comes responsibility, such as the knowledge of learning to be *Humble*. I felt like everything I claimed to be as an employee was being challenged by "the universe" which had led me to this very point in my life. I strongly felt that my decisions would lay the beginnings of my foundation in the workforce and set my path in the direction I chose from here on out. It felt as though this small window of opportunity to make a decision would set my fate and either show my gratitude to those who helped get me to this moment or it would be a slap in their faces. As a result, I decided to leave a good paying city job because I felt ethically challenged. This leap of faith was my answer back to the Universe. My answer was to choose my Purpose in Life over an Illusion of Fear. From then on, I decided that wherever the Universe guided me, I would trust the process. Then I remembered what I had already gone through in my life to get this far – how resilient I had become. A leap of faith? Well, here we go, once again!

I chose to stand my ground and made a sound decision based on the perfect alignment of my morals, my values, and my commitment to my ethics. Feeling proud that I didn't compromise my integrity for the sake of keeping a job, I pondered "What will happen when I finally follow through with my decision?" A reassurance came over me and answered, "Live."

Within the same week of settling on my decision, my cell phone rang. "Girl, come and get your check!" she said once I had answered.

"What check, Ms. B? Where in the world would I get a check?"

"Girl, if you don't come and get this check. You finished the program!" she said.

"Program…I'm confused. What are you talking about?" I asked out of frustration.

"The Family Self-Sufficiency program you signed up for, Toshar. The escrow account." She was trying to jar my memory.

"Oh, yes, I remember now. But wasn't that like five years ago?" I replied.

"Yes, and you are done with the program!" she went on.

"How much is the check for?" I asked, seriously doubting it was worth picking up in the first place.

"A little over $18,000!" I was dumbfounded. "Girl, you can put a down payment on a house if you want to!"

I was in shock. Never before had I saved that much money, willingly or unwillingly. And yet, here it was. My past self-had paid it forward to my future self. An overwhelming feeling of a reward for my choice washed over me. I had spoken and the Universe responded. Needless to say, I was able to stop working at ACS on my terms. Once I had decided ACS was no longer a good match for me as an employee, I received many calls from my coworkers telling me I was crazy to leave that job. I understood their concerns but knew something greater was in control. I knew they only saw the business side of me and didn't know of my struggle. They could only see the impossible happening to me, but I was used to this.

It was a good feeling to be able to spend quality time with my family for a couple of months. Just some time to think about life without the hustle and bustle of a routine that involved me getting up and going to work, playing on repeat every day. Of course, I still got up to look for employment. Although this time, it was not because I had to, but because I wanted to. The Universe was teaching me how to Live, and I was a sponge.

While enjoying my newly found freedom, I went to treat myself and enjoy some shopping. Opportunity came knocking in the form of a former coworker at New York Foundling whom I had bumped into. She told me that Visiting Nurse Services (VNS) was hiring. She was currently employed there and loved her job. I thanked the universe again for such an opportunity, applied for the job, and was hired immediately as a Clinical Case Manager.

VNS had a pilot program which worked with applicants and recipients of public assistance who were mandated to substance abuse treatment and also had multiple barriers (like domestic violence, child welfare, family issues, educational issues, etc.) to self-sufficiency. This entailed all of my work experiences wrapped up into one position, and I was more than happy to put all of it to good use.

Ms. Tara Mendizabal was the Associate Director of the program at that time and was exemplary of the workers she was recruiting. Tara made sure everyone's work was precise and services for the clients were well coordinated. Being part of this team meant that each team member was thorough and consistent in understanding the significant psychological, social, and emotional factors related to each client's recovery and vocational issues. We also functioned as the liaisons for our client's and other community agencies including housing, social services, medical providers, etc. In order to keep things in perspective, we prepared case presentations once per week to review and discuss during weekly team meetings. Yes, this position was all of my work experience rolled up into one, however, the pay was not going to propel me where my goals dictated me to be.

Once again opportunity came knocking, and my resume was READY!!! Life and living was good for me, and I was having a *GREAT TIME* at VNS. This was a place where you were valued as a worker and assessed on your work performance and your personality. This combination was important for me. Education was important as well, and VNS was willing to pay any employee's way through nursing school if one decided upon that particular career track. My options were endless, and the salary VNS paid their nurses was worth it.

Every year, May 5th is also known as Cinco de Mayo for some. It is a date in which Mexican troops were victorious against the French troops attempting to conquer them. Subsequently, the French did take over Mexico City. Nevertheless, May 5th is celebrated because of the Mexican's unity, determination, and pride in the face of overwhelming odds. However, for me, May 5,

2005 is when my Nana died. Nanny had a second stroke that left her in the hospital. On the day she passed, I remember waiting for the train during my lunch break while working for VNS. The air became silent, and in that moment, a bird flew past me. Later that night, I received a call from my mother telling me that Nanny had died around noon. Still protective of me, my family knew the best time to tell me was when they knew I was safe at home.

All I could remember was the fun Nanna and I had in life. During one of my hospital visits, she told me she was "tired of being here." To cheer her up, I said that I wouldn't buy flowers for her funeral, but instead I would bring flowers every time I visited her from that day forward. Her smart behind retorted, "How do you know you not going to go before me?" We laughed, hugged, and kissed as if each day was closer to the last day.

I can recall the very last time I visited Nanna, I brought her the most beautiful burnt orange roses. Before I could walk into her room, the nurse stopped me and sternly told me not to take the roses inside. I could not understand why, and she explained that

Nanna was not breathing on her own; she was on a respirator. I gave the flowers to the nurse to hold and proceeded into the room. My Nanna was unresponsive and I just looked out of the window as this was a scene too familiar for me to process. It was a bright afternoon. I could not bear to see Nanna lying in that hospital bed, so I just stared out of the window. It was that moment when rays of sunlight appeared to radiate from the sky down to the ground. This is also known as "Jacob's Ladder", a ladder to Heaven. The only way for me to cope with *THIS* was to be happy for her because she was no longer suffering. I had to constantly remind myself that Energy never dies – it *LIVES* on!

Shortly after this time, I received a call from a state job I had applied to as it literally paid double the salary I was earning at VNS. Not only that, it offered a union, unprecedented health benefits, and more! When I got the phone call informing me that I was hired, I knew I had reached my final goal in obtaining financial freedom from Section 8. I looked up into to the sky to give thanks and all I saw were the rays in the sky.

I was able to plan my transition off Section 8 to the point where I left my kids (who were now young adults) the Section 8 Voucher. I was preparing to move out because I had bought myself a house.

Over the years, I had kept all of my planners, so I took some time to review them while packing up my apartment. I gazed out of my Schomburg window and reminisced on each day I had accounted for in each planner. It was like traveling through time. I reviewed them all, taking note of my progress through the years and how the majority of the goals I had written down had been accomplished. No longer fearful, I was now confident and secure with my future. I then took pleasure writing in the closing date for my house. When I received the keys to my castle, I felt like a Queen.

Looking out of the window once again, I laughed at those times when I was braiding hair and finishing ten-page term papers during the darkest hours before dawn. I saw my reflection looking back at me and I had an epiphany – the past me was now looking at my Future Self. The realization served as more encouragement to step into my future, accomplish even bigger milestones, and continue moving forward as a strengthened individual.

***

I went through a dark forest filled with the thorns of a rose bush

I sweat my own blood, but still I had to push.

"Push towards the light," the voice said. "If you stay here you will die."

My fears were defeated by my courage when I saw the rays in the sky.

Let My Faith Guide You.......

How to Live

Some Thoughts by Faith

Be Free

- *Spend multiple nights out with family and friends without being displaced from the shelter for violating the 48-hour rule*
- *Take that vacation you weren't able to take - you're no longer required to report back to the shelter*

In order to live, you have to be free and feel free to do whatever makes you happy. You'll feel free not being chained down to being a statistic or less than. Imagine a life without the feeling of heavy weights on your shoulders or having to report to people who don't care about your well-being. Imagine having the ability to hang out with friends and family at your own leisure. It is a good feeling! Welfare officials will wonder how you were able to get yourself together because you are no longer trapped under their rules and regulations. Let them wonder!

Do you

- *Do what is best for you – continue to move forward to become a better you*
- *Build off of what you have (money, education, skills) – take the chance to become greater than what you were told you wouldn't become*
- *Give back to your community – volunteer, join groups that'll benefit society and fulfill you*

What is it that makes you love the person you are? Have you done anything lately that makes you better than before? Whenever I was able to attend, I joined dinner parties at church, and I was allowed to be myself and discuss how I felt about life, being sheltered, and put down. The hardships that I have endured will only serve to benefit my situation in the future.

Achieve

- *Now is the time to achieve those goals you weren't previously able to achieve*
- *Reward yourself for the stress and struggle you have overcome*
- *Set higher goals for your future, start building a stronger foundation, especially if you have children*
- *You can do anything you put your mind to!*

You know that car you wanted? That school you weren't able to attend? Go buy that car, go enroll in that school! Education is important, so I will continue to work towards a degree or certificates.

There are so many goals that I've wanted to achieve, and now I'm able to focus and accomplish them the proper way. Procrastination was a big habit of mine. I would be focused on so much and become overwhelmed which resulted in what can only be described as arrested development – a failure to move, act, and grow. Even the smallest goal, such as a raise at my job, needed to be rewarded so that I could continue forward with a positive attitude. I aim higher for myself because my children's future is dependent on what I achieve in the present.

You will get knocked down, but you will come back stronger. Just keep in mind that you can overcome anything if you are willing to put in the work.

Journal Your Experience

How do you plan to LIVE?

_____
_____
_____
_____
_____
_____
_____
_____
_____
_____
_____
_____
_____
_____
_____

Left to Right:

Me, Kim, My Mom and Our Babies

My Graduation at Hunter College

Yusef and Me

My Graduation at Hunter College

In Loving Memory of

My Nanna

Mattie Pearl

&

My Uncle Boo-Boo

www.ingramcontent.com/pod-product-compliance
Lightning Source LLC
Chambersburg PA
CBHW050650160426
43194CB00010B/1880